⬤ Smithsonian

LITTLE EXPLORER

ASTRONAUT IN TRAINING

by Kathryn Clay

raintree 🍃

a Capstone company — publishers for children

Raintree is an imprint of Capstone Global Library Limited, a company incorporated in England and Wales having its registered office at 264 Banbury Road, Oxford, OX2 7DY – Registered company number: 6695582

www.raintree.co.uk
myorders@raintree.co.uk

ISBN 978 1 4747 3303 8
21 20 19 18 17
10 9 8 7 6 5 4 3 2 1

British Library Cataloguing in Publication Data
A full catalogue record for this book is available from the British Library.

Editorial Credits
Arnold Ringstad, editor; Jake Nordby, designer and production specialist

Our very special thanks to Dr. Valerie Neal, Curator and Chair of the Space History Department at the Smithsonian National Air and Space Museum for her curatorial review. Capstone would also like to thank Kealy Gordon, Smithsonian Institution Product Development Manager, and the following at Smithsonian Enterprises: Christopher A. Liedel, President; Carol LeBlanc, Senior Vice President; Brigid Ferraro, Vice President; Ellen Nanney, Licensing Manager.

Acknowledgements
Alamy: NASA Photo, 20; AP Images: Rex Features/ESA-V. Crobu, 9; Dreamstime: Paul Hakimata, 10; Glow images: SuperStock, 1; NASA, 3, 4, 5 (middle), 5 (right), 8, 11 (top), 11 (bottom), 12 (top), 12 (bottom), 14, 15, 16, 17 (bottom right), 18–19, 21, 23, 24–25, 27 (top), 27 (bottom), 28–29, 30–31, Houston Chronicle, Smiley N. Pool, cover, B. Stafford, 12–13, Benny Benavides, 28, Bill Ingalls, 19, Joel Kowsky, 22; Newscom: Blend Images/Hill Street Studios, 6 (left); Science Source: Allen Green, 17 (top right), Publiphoto, 26, RIA Novosti, 5 (left); Shutterstock: Kolo, 17, LOVEgraphic, 24, MarcelClemens, 32, pio3, 27 (background)

Design Elements: Shutterstock Images: Ovchinnkov Vladimir, Shay Yacobinski, Teneresa

Printed and bound in China.

CONTENTS

WHO ARE ASTRONAUTS?

The first astronauts launched into space in 1961. Since then many people have travelled to space. A few of them flew to the Moon. But most stay near the Earth.

Astronauts eat, sleep and work in space.

Yuri Gagarin

Neil Armstrong

Tim Peake

FAMOUS ASTRONAUTS

name	country	first mission	previous job
Yuri Gagarin	Soviet Union	1961	military pilot
Valentina Tereshkova	Soviet Union	1963	skydiver/factory worker
Neil Armstrong	United States	1966	test pilot/engineer
Sally Ride	United States	1983	physicist
Chris Hadfield	Canada	1995	military pilot/engineer
Tim Peake	United Kingdom	2015	military pilot

Early astronauts were pilots. Most were in the military. Today other kinds of people can be astronauts too. Many are scientists. Some are engineers. All astronauts face tough training.

5

BECOMING AN ASTRONAUT

Becoming an astronaut is competitive. A university degree is a must. Future astronauts study science and engineering. The space agency NASA chooses and trains U.S. astronauts.

Astronauts must be healthy and physically fit. They need excellent eyesight. They face a difficult interview process.

Students who want to become astronauts must study hard in school.

ASTRONAUT REQUIREMENTS

These are just a few of the many requirements for becoming a NASA astronaut.

- [ ] height between 157 and 191 centimetres (62–75 inches)

- [ ] blood pressure 140/90 or lower

- [ ] three years of professional experience after gaining a university degree, or 1,000 hours of experience flying jets

- [ ] swimming test, showing astronauts can survive if their spacecraft lands in water

BASIC TRAINING

U.S. astronauts train in Houston, Texas, U.S.A. Astronauts from other nations train in their home countries and in the United States. They spend years preparing. They learn the skills they need for space missions.

Astronauts have trained at the Johnson Space Center in Houston since the 1960s.

Survival skills are important too. A spacecraft could land in a remote area. Astronauts learn how to treat injuries. They learn how to build shelters and find clean water.

Astronauts Tim Peake (right) and Samantha Cristoforetti prepare dinner over a fire during survival training.

Training for a space mission is a long process. Italian Astronaut Roberto Vittori explains that the training feels like a journey itself. He says, "In some ways, our space flight is as much the end of a long journey as it is the beginning of a new one."

ADVANCED TRAINING

Many astronauts study the International Space Station (ISS). It will be their home in space. They learn about its different parts and rooms. Full-sized models let them practise moving through the ISS.

A huge space station model is based in Houston, Texas, U.S.A.

Astronauts work with Russian cosmonauts. They learn the Russian language and customs. The cosmonauts learn English. They all train together in Houston and Star City, Russia.

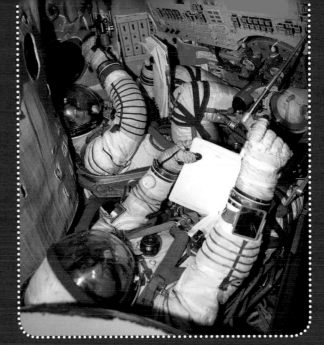

An astronaut (top) and cosmonaut (bottom) train together in Star City.

THE INTERNATIONAL SPACE STATION

The ISS is a science lab in space! Countries around the world worked together to build it. The ISS circles Earth every 90 minutes. By 2016 more than 200 people from 18 countries had visited it.

PREPARING FOR SPACEWALKS

Astronauts sometimes leave their spacecraft. This is called a spacewalk. Spacewalk training is done underwater. Astronauts can float and move like they will in space.

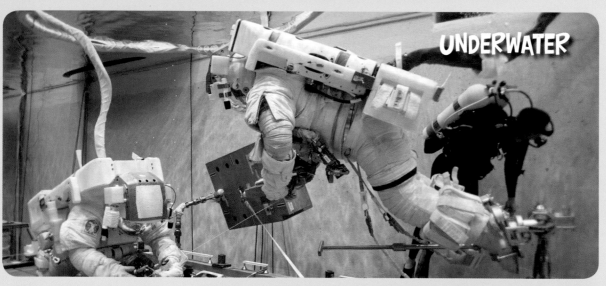

UNDERWATER

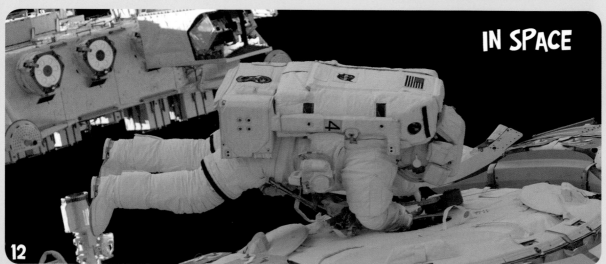

IN SPACE

Astronauts practise water survival skills. They also have diving lessons. They must be strong swimmers.

UNDERWATER TRAINING

The NASA centre in Houston has a giant pool. Inside are full-sized models of spacecraft. Astronauts practise with the tools they will use in space.

WEIGHTLESSNESS

Astronaut Robert Satcher floats during weightlessness training.

Astronauts train for weightlessness, or floating in space. They go up in aeroplanes that fly in large upside-down U shapes. Passengers feel weightless and float around for about 25 seconds. The plane does this up to 60 times during one flight.

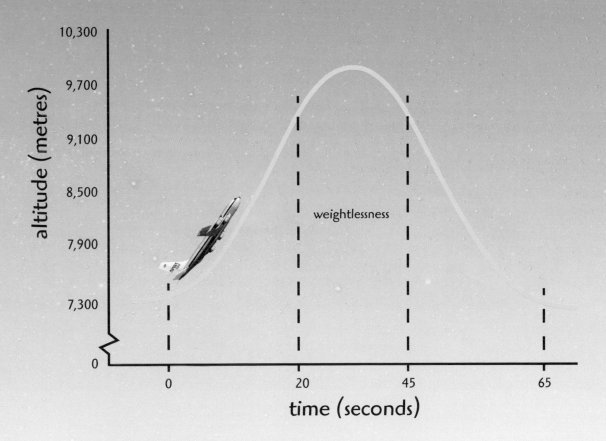

This training makes many people experience motion sickness. The aeroplanes are nicknamed "vomit comets."

PRACTISING WITH MODELS

The main U.S. spacecraft from 1981 to 2011 was the space shuttle. It looked like a jet aircraft. Shuttle training happened in Houston.

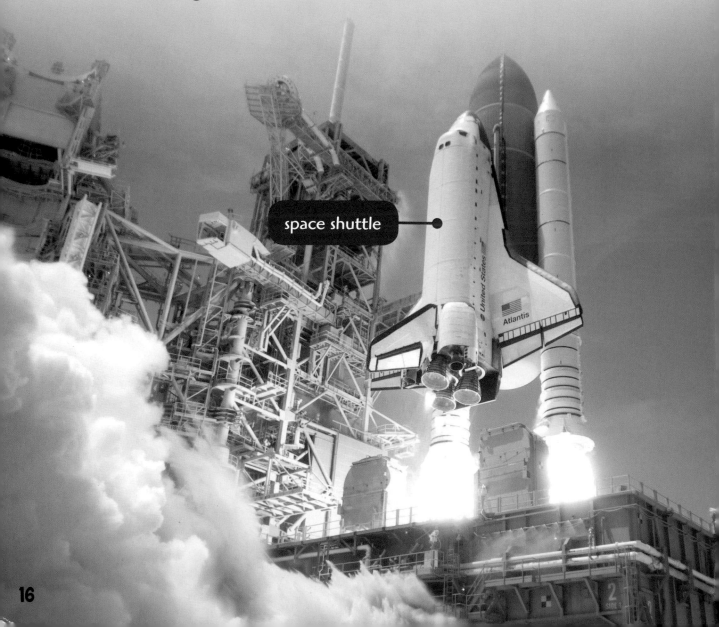

space shuttle

Astronauts trained using full-sized models of the space shuttle. Models could tilt upwards to practise launches. They could tilt downwards to practise landings. Space shuttle astronauts spent more than 300 hours in the model before a flight.

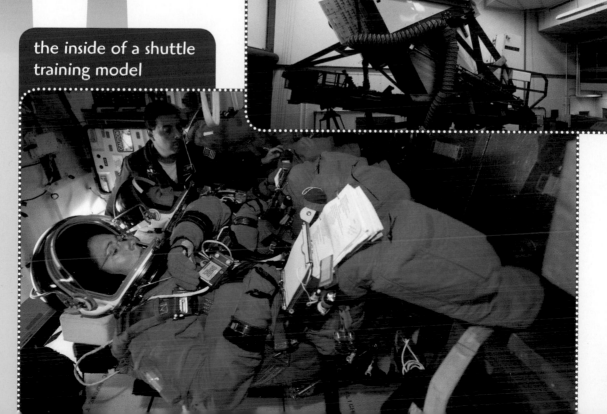

the outside of a shuttle training model

the inside of a shuttle training model

THE SOYUZ SPACECRAFT

The space shuttle was retired in 2011. Now all astronauts travel in small Russian spacecraft. These are called Soyuz. In English, *Soyuz* means "union." Each spacecraft holds three people.

supply spacecraft

a Soyuz spacecraft attached to the International Space Station

Astronauts practise in a Soyuz model. The model is in Russia.

SPACE GEAR

Wearing a space suit is no easy task. The suits are bulky to keep astronauts safe. Putting on a suit can take about 45 minutes!

Astronauts must be comfortable in their suits before missions. They learn how to put on each piece. Then they practise moving and working in the suits. Each task is practised many times before a mission.

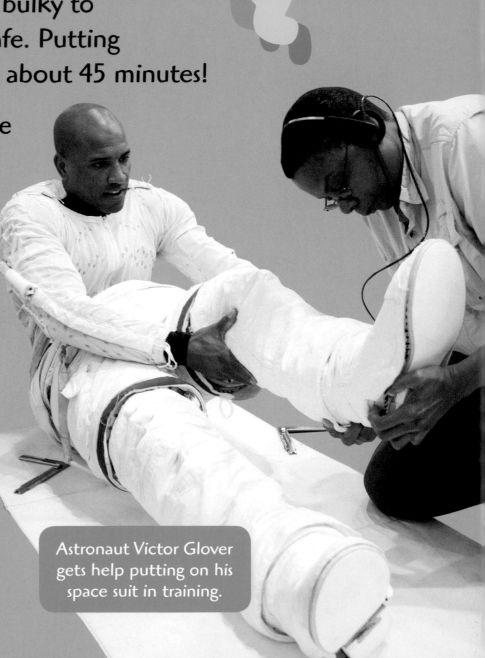

Astronaut Victor Glover gets help putting on his space suit in training.

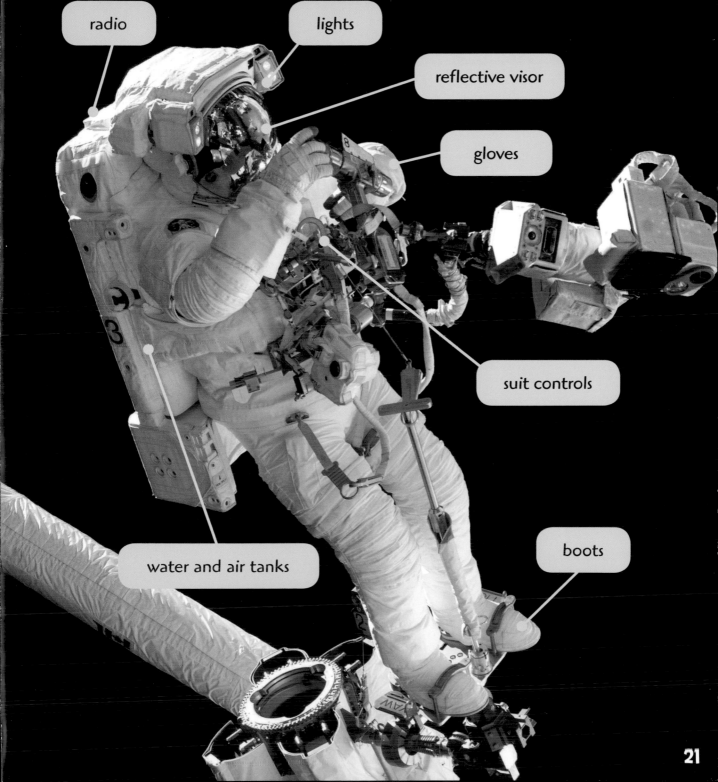

radio

lights

reflective visor

gloves

suit controls

water and air tanks

boots

21

MISSION TRAINING

Astronauts are assigned to different missions. Mission training can take up to three years. Astronauts learn details about their missions. Each astronaut has a special job.

A crew stands in front of their rocket before a mission.

Everyone learns the skills they need. Some may build or repair parts of the space station. Others may work on science experiments. The crew trains together. They practise working as a team.

A crew goes over the plans for an upcoming mission.

TRAINING WITH MISSION CONTROL

Mission control supports the astronauts. Workers there are called flight controllers. Astronauts and flight controllers practise their missions together.

The U.S. mission control centre is in Houston. The European centre is in Darmstadt, Germany. The Russian centre is in Korolev, Russia.

Darmstadt, Germany

Korolev, Russia

Houston, Texas

Flight controllers try to think of any problems that might happen. Solving problems on the ground prepares them for success.

Flight controllers can see information about the spacecraft. They pass along this information to the crew. They work to keep the crew safe.

THE FUTURE OF ASTRONAUT TRAINING

Astronauts travelled to the Moon in the 1960s and 1970s. They have not travelled to other planets yet. But that may soon change. Today's astronauts are training for the missions of the future.

The astronauts of tomorrow may explore Mars.

Orion
crew module

Orion service module
(holds engines and supplies)

The United States is building a new type of spacecraft called Orion. It will travel far into space. Astronauts might even land on Mars. The mission will bring many challenges. Astronauts study these challenges on the ISS.

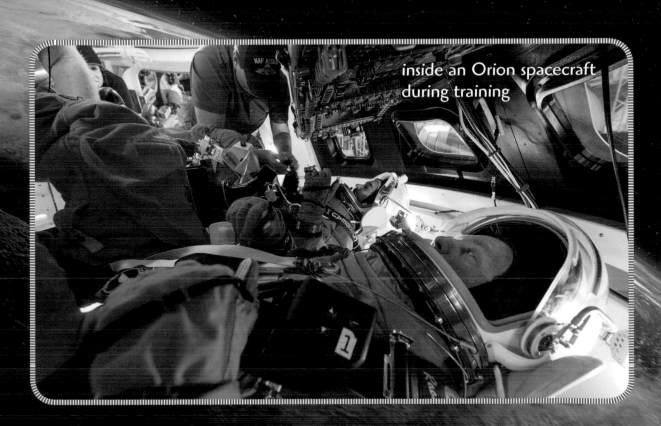

inside an Orion spacecraft during training

A TOUGH AND REWARDING JOB

Training for space travel isn't easy. Astronauts push their minds and bodies to the limit. They risk their lives on dangerous missions.

However astronauts say the hard work is worth it. They get to see Earth from space. They do important scientific work. And they work alongside other space travellers. All this is made possible by the astronauts' intense training.

An astronaut crew stands inside a training model.

Astronaut John Grunsfeld gives a thumbs-up in space.

GLOSSARY

blood pressure force of blood as it flows through a person's body

competitive involving many different people struggling to win or succeed

cosmonaut Russian astronaut

custom tradition in a culture or society

engineer person who designs, builds and improves things

intense difficult and requiring a lot of energy and effort

model something that is made to look like a person, animal or object

pilot person who flies aircraft

remote far from other things

spacecraft craft built to travel in space

weightlessness feeling of not being pulled down toward Earth

COMPREHENSION QUESTIONS

1. How do astronauts train for spacewalks? Where do they do this training?

2. Astronauts must be very healthy. Why is it important for people who fly into space to be healthy?

3. Page 17 shows the inside and outside of a spacecraft model used for training. How does seeing both the inside and outside help you understand how this training tool works?

READ MORE

Ground Control to Major Tim: A Biography of Tim Peake, Clive Gifford (Wayland, 2017).

The Story of Space: Space Stations, Steve Parker (Franklin Watts, 2015).

The Usborne Official Astronaut's Handbook (Handbooks), Louie Stowell (author), Roger Simo (illustrator) (Usborne Publishing Limited, 2015).

WEBSITES

BBC: Tim Peake
www.bbc.co.uk/timelines/z2gxp39
Explore how Tim Peake became an astronaut.

ESA: Astronaut Training
www.esa.int/esaKIDSen/SEM3RIWJD1E_LifeinSpace_0.html
Learn more about how ESA astronauts prepare to launch into space.

Tim Peake's Blog
blogs.esa.int/tim-peake/
Read about Tim Peake's experiences in space.

INDEX